Memories of Bygone Oxford Shops

Hazel Bleay

ROBERT BOYD PUBLICATIONS

Published by
Robert Boyd Publications
260 Colwell Drive
Witney, Oxon OX28 5LW

Copyright © Hazel Bleay

First Published 2010

ISBN: 978 1 899536 95 5

Printed and bound by Information Press
Southfield Road, Eynsham
Oxford OX29 4JB

Contents

Dedication

I would like to dedicate this book of my memories of bygone shops of Oxford to my late mother-in-law Mrs Eva Bleay, and to my late husband, Sid Bleay.

Acknowledgements

I would like to thank all those who have helped me with this book especially Malcolm Graham and Stephen Rench of the Oxfordshire County Council Photographic Archives for their help and written permission to use the photographs, also especially Nuala La Vertue who printed the copies of the photographs of the old shops of Oxford for me.

My thanks are also due to the following people, Mr John Mutton for allowing me to obtain copies of his photographs of G R Cooper's of Castle Street, also for the excerpt of his working life in this shop.

Mr David Newton and Simon Newton of Darke and Taylor for the photographs and history of Hill Upton of George Street.

Lloyds Bank in High Street for allowing me to photograph the tiles in their office downstairs which were originally in Sainsbury's shop next door, and was incorporated in the extended premises of the bank in 1974.

Mr Tony Taylor for information of his late father Reg Taylor who worked at Grimbly Hughes in Cornmarket Street.

Pam Clements for the photograph of her grandfather, Alfred E Alder, who drove the van belonging to Badcocks of Queen Street.

Carol Milward for the copy of her husband Geoff's photograph of Milwards staff in the shoe shop in Cornmarket Street where his mother worked.

Mr Brian Lowe who loaned me a book and gave me encouragement to write this book.

Bob and Isobel of Duckers in the Turl for their help and information of this lovely old business, still making hand made shoes.

Mr Stephen Pritchard and Mary Faulkner of Rowles in the Turl for their helpful information on the history of Rowles, which started in the High in 1797.

Judy Payne of Payne and Sons for her help about this old established family firm, in business in the High Street for seven generations.

David Marcus and daughter Caroline of Reginald Davis of High Street for their helpful information.

Mrs Julia Smith for deciphering my writing and producing the first typewritten draft. I am most grateful as I nearly gave up the idea, as trying to print on a computer was taking me a long time - I am too old for this new technology.

I would also like to thank my two daughters Jane and Sally who encouraged me to write this book of my memories of all the lovely old shops that have disappeared from Oxford.

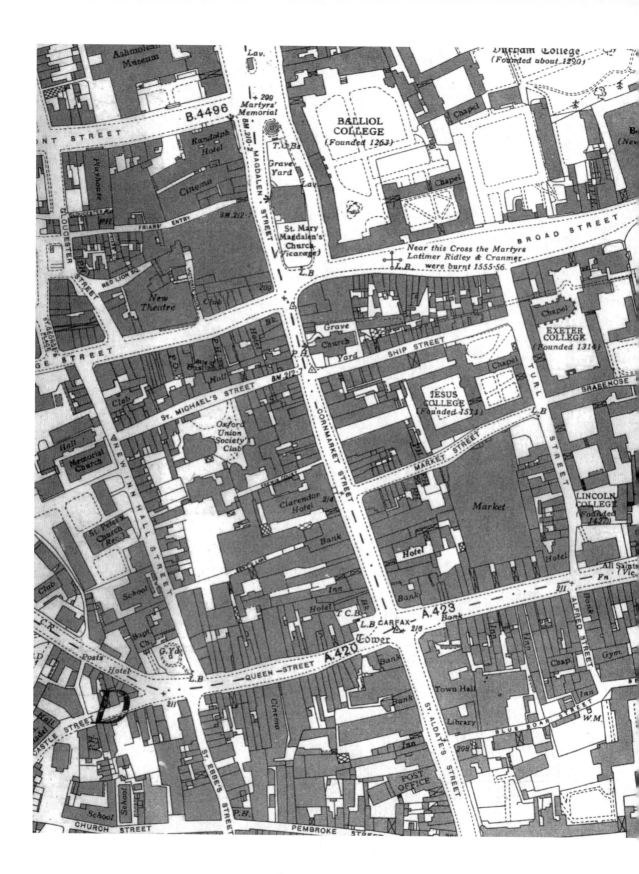

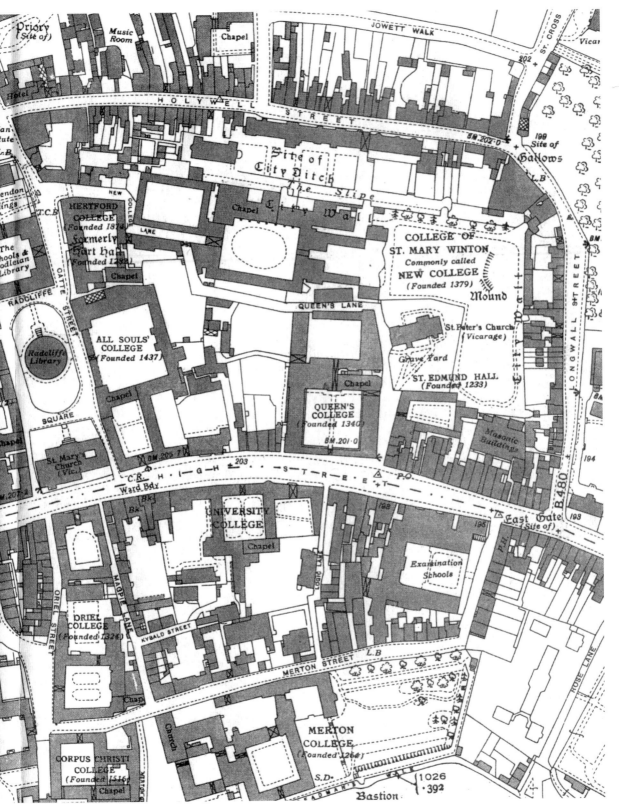

Map of Oxford City Centre c. 1947.

Preface

When I was a child I never owned a dolls house. After my husband died eight years ago I decided that I would like to start a new hobby. My youngest daughter took me to my first dolls house fair and I bought my first dolls house. I enjoyed decorating and furnishing it.

I then bought a dolls house kit of a cottage - one up and one down, very much like the one I had lived in when I was first married. This cottage, called Fern Cottage, was located in Old Marston, Oxford. Sadly it was demolished in the late 1950s as it was condemned. I decorated and furnished my dolls house kit exactly as I had remembered Fern Cottage.

My next dolls house kit was a shop, and, whilst wondering what kind of shop to do, I remembered the lovely cake shop and café called The Cadena in Cornmarket Street, Oxford. This was the inspiration that gave me the idea of writing this book "Memories of Bygone Oxford Shops".

I am very proud of this beautiful city, with its colleges and parks, especially Christchurch College and Christchurch Meadow, and feel privileged to have spent my life surrounded by this beauty. Before my memories fade away I would like to remember the old Oxford shops that have disappeared, and hope to rekindle some happy memories for both Oxford residents and others who may find them interesting. This book is about my memories and is therefore not a definitive work - its pure nostalgia!

CHAPTER 1

Personal Memories

I was born Hazel Phipps on 9th February 1931, the only daughter of Cyril and Grace Phipps.

I attended school at East Oxford in Union Street off Cowley Road. This was a girls' school and the boys' school was separate, but by the time my brother, Michael Phipps, who was twelve years younger than me, attended this school it had become a mixed school. My late husband, Sid Bleay, lived in Alma Place, off Cowley Road, and also went to East Oxford School.

I met Sid when I was twelve years old and we both left school at the age of fourteen. We lost touch for about four years, as Sid joined the Coldstream Guards when he was just seventeen and a half. In September 1948 Sid returned from Palestine and was stationed at the Tower of London. On a Sunday evening we met by chance at the bus stop next to the Friar Pub at Marston, near to the grocery and greengrocers shop, kept by Sid's parents, Fred and Eva Bleay. His period of leave had finished, and he was returning by train to the Tower of London. He asked if I remembered him, I said yes, and that was it – the spark was still there.

We arranged to meet the following weekend at the Carfax Assembly Rooms in Cornmarket Street, a well known Oxford venue for ballroom dancing, which was very poplar in the 1940s and 50s. Dance bands popular at that time were Stan Rogers and the Blue Star Players, also Eric Tolly and his group, and Ricky Derges. Stan was a local man whose father and mother had a shop in Commercial Road in St Ebbes. These musicians also played for ballroom dancing at the Town Hall and the Forum in The High Street, also the Holyoake Hall in Headington. The Holyoake has now been developed into flats. The Carfax Assembly Rooms was where everybody met on a Saturday night - no drunken brawls or fights in those days, just people enjoying the dancing and each others company. Happy memories.

My eldest daughter Jane used to go dancing at the Carfax Assembly Rooms in the 1960s, but sadly Cornmarket Street started to change, with the lovely old buildings and shops being demolished to make way for the shopping arcade to be built - the Clarendon Centre, named after the Clarendon Hotel which was also demolished. The Carfax Assembly Rooms were no more; this grand building was incorporated with the HSBC Bank on the corner of Carfax and Cornmarket Street.

How Oxford has changed since I married in 1949 is unbelievable! The famous old shops have gone; Capes of St Ebbes, G R Cooper's, Badcocks in Queen Street, Webbers and Sainsbury's in The High, Grimbly Hughes and Woolworths and the Cadena Café and Fullers in Cornmarket and many more.

The photographs in this book will, hopefully, bring back happy memories of the lovely old shops of Oxford that have disappeared.

Mr Jimmy Dingle was a famous Oxford character with his billboard advertising local businesses and events. Jimmy died in 1970, aged 84

CHAPTER TWO

Memories of bygone shops

On leaving school at the age of fourteen I was apprenticed to learn hairdressing with Mr Lionel Harrison of Harrisons in Queens Street, within Barratt Chambers over Barratts the shoe shop. Apprentices did not receive a large wage, the first year I earned 5 shillings a week, the second year was 10 shillings and the third year was 15 shillings. You did get tips from the customers, which helped greatly, and of course you did learn a trade. I wonder what the young people of today would think of that amount these days? Mr Harrison was a good boss to work for, and he became the Mayor of Oxford a few years later.

Barratts shoe shop, at 38 Queen Street, was next door to Crawfords restaurant, with Colliers the men's tailors, known as Fifty Shilling Tailors, underneath. The other side of Barratts was the Co-op Dairy and café and Timothy Whites the Chemist. These buildings were demolished in 1984 to make the entrance into the new Clarendon shopping arcade, which goes through to the other entrance in Cornmarket Street, with an exit via Shoe Lane into New Inn Hall Street.

Opposite Harrisons was Badcocks, a wonderful store which sold beautiful material. It was here that I bought the material for my wedding dress, also material for my three bridesmaids' dresses, made by Miss Bossom, a friend of my mothers.

Badcocks also sold good quality clothes and hats etc., the staff were always very helpful. When Badcocks closed it was taken over by the Oxford Co-op.

Marks & Spencers occupied large premises in Cornmarket Street, opposite the Cadena Café. In March 1978 they exchanged premises with the Oxford Co-op, eventually moving to new premises in Queen Street, where they are still trading. Unfortunately the striking frontage of Badcocks was demolished with the building of the new Marks & Spencer shop. The Oxford Co-op moved to Cornmarket, into the former premises of Marks & Spencer. On the lower floor they opened a large grocery store.

My wedding ring came from Ballards, the jewellers at the top of Queen Street near Carfax tower. These premises are now occupied by Crabtree and Evelyn, who began trading here in 1982. My engagement ring was bought from Pleasance and Harpers Limited at 3 George Street, another jeweller that has disappeared.

Sid and I were married on Boxing Day 1949 at St Nicholas Church in Old Marston, and moved into Fern Cottage in Old Marston Village, near the White Hart public house. Together we went to Webbers shop in the High Street, Webbers was a department store selling fashions, household items and had a children's department which sold school uniforms for many local schools. They also had a furniture department where in 1949, just before we were married, Sid and I bought our dining room suite and a bed. The bed was marked with the utility sign, a feature of wartime furniture which was in limited supply. In those days you had to save up and pay cash, credit was not easily available. Also in the High Street was Mintys, a local furniture shop which had a factory in Cherwell Street off St Clements where we bought two rocking chairs. The furniture was very well made by local tradesmen.

Before my eldest daughter was born in December 1950, I left my job as a hairdresser and went to work at Grimbly Hughes in Cornmarket Street, a high class grocery store which was established in 1840. This grocery and wine shop was famous for its large selection of cheese and bacon. In their wholesale department in St Michael's Hall in Shoe Lane off New Inn Hall Street, they had a smoke house where they smoked sides of bacon, and rashers were sliced to the thickness preferred by the customer. The rashers were very tasty and did not shrink or spatter when cooked as they do today.

I worked at Grimbly Hughes part time for six months, first in the packing room, then I was offered a position to work on the cheese and bacon counter. I worked with two lovely gentlemen, one man was called Sam, but I cannot remember his surname. The other man was Reg Taylor who had worked at Grimbly Hughes straight from school, the Oxford Boys Grammar school in George Street. He worked at Grimbly Hughes until the shop closed and then went to work at Aldens at the corner of Oakthorpe Road in Summertown. Reg Taylor was born in 1907 and worked until he was 80 and lived until the age of 97; a very active man and well liked. I am so proud to have known him in the 1950s. Both Reg and Sam were very kind and supportive to me as I had never worked in a shop before.

Grimbly Hughes was a very pleasant shop to work in and the staff and managers were all very nice. Grimbly's had a large packing department for customer orders and had their own fleet of vans which used to deliver the customers shopping, mostly to the north Oxford area, Banbury Road and Woodstock Road, also Boars Hill and the Cumnor area. Grimbly Hughes also had branches in Bedford and Leamington Spa. Sadly Grimbly Hughes closed when Cornmarket was in the process of change; most grocery shops including Twinings, Maypole, Liptons, Home and Colonial, and the International Stores closed when the large supermarkets began trading.

All these unique shops, each with their own character, have disappeared from the streets of Oxford.

CHAPTER THREE

My favourite Oxford Shops

Cadena Café

One of my favourite shops that I best remember in Oxford was the Cadena Café in Cornmarket Street, where my aunt, Mrs Maud Alright, was the manageress of the cakes and bread shop. The Cadena sold wedding cakes also Christmas cakes and, at Easter, they sold simnel cakes and a variety of small cakes. They had their own bakery in Mill Street, Osney. My aunt had a Christening cake made for my eldest daughter Jane, the decoration on the top of the cake was a stork carrying a small baby doll in its beak. Also when Jane was three years old my aunt had a birthday cake made with three Micky Mouse china candle holders. We still have these Micky Mouse holders.

The Cadena was a lovely shop and restaurant and I remember the smell of the coffee beans being roasted in the basement, wafting up through the grid below the windows at the front of the shop as you walked by. A most delicious smell, which tempted you to stop and buy either coffee beans which were ground for you fresh from the shop, or to go into the café on the ground floor for a cup of their lovely coffee.

My late mother-in-law Eva Bleay used to take me to the restaurant for afternoon tea for a special treat before I was married. The restaurant was upstairs and I can remember a lady playing a cello and a gentleman dressed in his dress suit playing the piano, very posh, with nice china tea cups and saucers, not mugs like today and a three tier cake stand with an assortment of gorgeous small cakes to choose from. The restaurant was also used for wedding receptions. In 1950 Jimmy Dingle and his bride held their wedding reception upstairs in the Cadena, see page 78. Jimmy Dingle was one of Oxford's famous characters, always very smartly dressed in top hat and tails and white spats on his shoes, with his billboard advertising sales in the local shops, also exhibitions being held in the Oxford town hall in St Aldates. Sometimes he would advertise dances to be held at the Carfax Assembly Rooms in Cornmarket, and the Holyoake Hall in Headington.

When the Cadena closed this lovely old shop with its old fashioned frontage it was demolished to make way for the not so pretty new building which you can see today. The new shop was a material shop called Gordon Thody Fabrics. It had three floors of materials, paper patterns and haberdashery. My youngest daughter, Sally, bought the material for her three bridesmaids' dresses in 1974. This shop is also now closed and the premises are occupied by HMV selling videos, CDs etc. Cornmarket Street has changed dramatically since the 1950s, now it is all take-aways, coffee bars, burger bars and other fast food outlets who's packaging often ends up on the streets of this lovely city.

F Cape & Co

In St Ebbes was another favourite shop of mine. Capes was an old fashioned shop loved by all the older residents of Oxford. It was a departmental shop selling haberdashery, ladies corsets, underwear and hosiery, also furniture including Lloyd Loom chairs and linen baskets, which were popular in the 1930's and 40's. When my late mother-in-law died I inherited a Lloyd Loom chair from her which I still possess.

I used to visit Capes with my two small daughters to buy my grandmother thick lisle stocking which she liked for Christmas, also small children's handkerchiefs, and sewing boxes filled with cottons, pins and sewing needles, also scissors, knitting wool and knitting needles to put into my small daughters Christmas stockings. It was like Aladdin's Cave inside this lovely old shop, and, at Christmas time, decorations would be strung across St Ebbes Street, which made it a magical place to visit.

My daughters were fascinated by the cash railway. The money was put into a container by the assistant and travelled on a wire across the shop, overhead to the cash desk, then the change was returned in the container back to the assistant for the customer. There was always a chair by the counter for customers to use, mostly a bentwood chair as shown in the Capes photographs. This courtesy was also available in Badcocks which I mention later in this book.

My late mother-in-law, Eva Bleay of Marston, worked in Capes in St Ebbes when she was young and, after Capes closed, my husband Sid and I took her to Woodstock Museum to see the exhibition of F Cape and Co. She was thrilled; it brought back very happy memories for her. In the Oxford Museum on the corner of Blue Boar Street in St Aldates there is still a small exhibition of Capes shop, with the counter and haberdashery fittings and shelves.

In the photograph of Capes office in Chapter 7, is a friend of my late mother-in-law, Mrs Goodey, who worked at Capes until the shop closed. Note the old fashion adding machine being used by Mrs Goodey. The other photograph shows the wall clock, advertising Fitu Corsets. F Cape and Co also had two other shops, one in Walton Street the other in Cowley Road.

Mac Fisheries

Another shop that I used to visit with my two daughters was Mac Fisheries on the corner of Castle Street and New Road, at the bottom end of Queen Street. They had a tank with live fish swimming in for customers to choose their fish from. This shop was demolished when the Westgate Shopping Centre was built and the Oxford City Library is now built close to this site. A photograph of Mac Fisheries is in chapter 6.

G R Cooper

G R Cooper was an interesting shop to visit in Queen Street. There was an ironmongers department, also paint and wallpaper, and a large gardening department in the basement. This store was unique, another shop like Aladdin's cave. In the 1950s when my two daughters were small we always went to visit Father Christmas in his grotto in the basement and received a small present wrapped in pink paper for girls and blue paper for boys. At Christmas the shop was decorated very tastefully. Cooper's was a good place to shop with a lot of character and very helpful staff.

Mr John Mutton was a good friend of my late husband, Sid. Mr Mutton worked at Cooper's from when he was 14 until he retired, and he wrote a short "History of G R Cooper's", from which I quote below:

"The ironmongery business of G R Cooper's was established in the 19th Century and thrived well enough to acquire neighbouring premises at St Ebbes corner until, by the 1930's, it had become by far the largest specialist hardware department store in Great Britain, operating on three sales floors It is still remembered with fond affection, not only for its wooden floors, but mostly for its unique brand of services and knowledgeable helpful staff, some of whom were trained to national diploma standards.

From Cooper's vast variety of stock you could buy an ounce of nails, a couple of screws, a tap washer, a complete calor gas installation, an aga cooker, a motor mower, a gallon of paraffin, wicks and glass chimney for paraffin lamps, and a four penny packet of seeds - with expert advice on all these items. You could have your tent repaired, your bike mended, your tin kettle soldered and a wooden roller made to measure for your mangle. G R Cooper's had a large fleet of vans and open lorries which delivered free within a 30 mile radius.

After World War II and after post war restrictions petered out, Cooper's like other de-partment stores was swept along by the boom years of the 1950s and 60s. By this time St Ebbes corner became due for redevelopment and the Westgate Centre was conceived and born. Cooper's business and premises plus extra land leased from Oxford City Council was acquired by Selfridges of Oxford Street London in April 1966 who built a fine new department store covering the whole of St Ebbes corner. Ironmongery and hardware still featured strongly, but the predominance now was for fashion, cosmetics, toys, furniture, TV and audio.

As retailing patterns changed, so did ownership of many retail businesses and in the early 90's the St Ebbes corner site was acquired by among others - Owen and Owen, then Alders, now Primark."

I am most indebted to John Mutton who started work as a sales assistant and was a personnel manager by the time he retired. Mr Mutton provided me with much information on G R Cooper and also allowed me to use his photographs of Cooper's' art deco building, and the photograph of the new building when Selfridges took over the premises during the construction of the Westgate Centre. These photographs are shown in chapter 6.

CHAPTER 4

High Street

High Street North side, from Longwall Street (see map on pages 6 and 7)
Some of the old shops that have disappeared.

No 57 Braziers - house furniture and interior decorators.
No 56 Gillman & Soame - a well known photographers.
No 55 C Wright - furriers
No 52 W P Hine & Co - tailors
No 51 Roland Bennett - jewellers

The next building is shown on the map as Masonic Buildings. This was the Forum Restaurant which was used for Wedding Receptions and for Ballroom Dancing. I was married on Boxing Day, December 1949, and we held our wedding reception here. It was a beautiful room and had a very grand staircase, with an excellent location at the bottom of the stairs for wedding photographs. Every Saturday evening there were ballroom dances held here with local dance bands, it had a spacious dance floor. The last dance took place on 16 June 1965, after which this building was demolished for an extension to St Edmunds Hall for extra student accommodation. The entrance at the front of this old Masonic building - then the Forum - is still there. It is a curved arch with metal gates which is now used by the students for pedestrian entry to St Edmunds Hall. Above the window is the college crest, a shield with a coat of arms. Another part of Oxford history that has disappeared.

No 50 W Ridler - antique dealer
No 48 Audley Miller - antique shop.
No 46 Wymans & Sons - bookseller
No 44-45 Minty Ltd - a well known shop selling furniture made at their factory in
    Cave Street.
No 41 a café called The Copper Kettle

No 40 Culpeper House – herbalist dealing with medicinal herbs. This shop is now incorporated with no 41 into a larger café, called Queens Lane Coffee House, popular with Oxford students and tourists.

No 38 K Williams - hairdresser. It is still a men's hairdresser and is called High Street Barbers.

No 37 John Rogers Ltd - established 1875, watch maker and jewellers. I used to take my watch to be cleaned and repaired here, and also bought a silver charm for my silver charm bracelet. The charm was in the shape of a camera and the view through the small lens showed a picture of Oxford High Street. This was unique and made especially for John Rogers. Sadly this shop has closed, another of Oxfords shops that is no longer in existence. This shop is now a tobacconist, Frederick Tranter.

No 34 Reginald Davis - antique jewellery and silver, also valuer for insurance purposes. This is still a family business run by David Marcus and his daughter Caroline, the third generation. David Marcus's great grandfather came from London in 1839. When Webbers in The High Street closed in 1971 David's father bought a counter from them which is still in use today. Reginald Davis is still in business today with very helpful staff.

No 23 Rymans & Co Ltd - sold artists materials and picture frames. This shop has closed.

No 20 Leslie Davey & West Ltd - jewellers and silversmiths. In the 1950s and 60s gold or silver link charm bracelets were very popular. When my husband and I and our two daughters went away for a week's holiday, mostly to Weymouth or Devon or Cornwall, I would buy a silver charm to remember the places we visited. In Clovelly I bought a donkey and in Plymouth a charm showing Francis Drake with bowls. For my silver wedding anniversary my husband bought me a charm of a church which opened showing people inside. Happy memories. Leslie Davey & West closed in recent years.

After passing Turl Street, the Mitre Hotel is a very prominent building. This was originally an old coaching inn. Today it is no longer a hotel but a restaurant, very popular with tourists when they visit Oxford.

No 9-15 Webbers Ltd - a well known large department shop. Webbers occupied a large site in front of the Covered Market for more than 60 years, from 1905 until it closed in 1971, when the store was split into a number of separate shops. The upper frontage, however, was saved and can be seen in the photographs in this chapter. Webbers was a lovely shop, selling ladies fashions, hats, children's and baby clothes and equipment, also curtain and materials and furniture. In the basement there was a household and kitchen department, in the photograph on page 24 can be seen enamel bread bins, also cake and flour bins which are still being manufactured today, and are apparently back in fashion! I had a cream and green enamel bread bin and flour bin as a wedding present.

No 8 S King & Son – a small shop selling beautiful china and glassware also canteens of cutlery.

No 6-7 the International Stores grocery shop.

No 4-5 J Sainsbury Ltd – a shop with many separate counters selling groceries, cheese and bacon also meat and chicken and, in the weeks before Christmas, lots of extras - Christmas cakes and puddings, hampers, turkeys, geese and gammon joints. This shop had striking tiles on the walls and floor. Sainsbury's closed and part of this shop and the building above was taken over by Lloyds Bank next door. The bank still have part of the tiles in one of their downstairs offices. Sainsbury's are of course, still trading in Oxford, and are now located at the back end of the Westgate centre with an entrance leading into St Ebbes, a smaller shop has also been opened in Magdalen Street. The original Sainsbury's site in the High Street is now occupied by Rymans, a stationers, popular with Oxford students. In the photograph of Sainsbury's, with Carfax Tower in the background (see page 25), there is a shop called Gill & Co next to Sainsbury's. This ironmongery shop later moved to the other side of High Street, next door to Kendall & Sons, eventually moving to smaller premises in Wheatsheaf Yard, off the High Street. Gills are still trading from these premises.

The tiled wall retained in the offices of Lloyds Bank.

The Masonic Buildings in High Street were used for casualties of World War I servicemen, patients can be seen standing outside the entrance. The 3rd General Hospital had its headquarters in various buildings around the city, including a surgical ward in the Examination School, opposite the Masonic Buildings.

Looking down High Street just beyond Queens Lane, on the left is Culpeper House, herbalists, and beyond, the former premises of Minty, a quality furniture shop which operated from 1887-1992.

Looking up the High Street towards Carfax, on the right is the Mitre Hotel, formerly a coaching inn. No longer a hotel but a very popular restaurant.

Almost at the top of High Street looking down is department store Webbers which traded between 1905 and 1971. Between their shop fronts were the entrance avenues to the covered market.

A pre-war Webbers delivery van complete with smartly uniformed drivers.

An extravagant looking acknowledgement of a valued order on Webbers letterheaded paper.

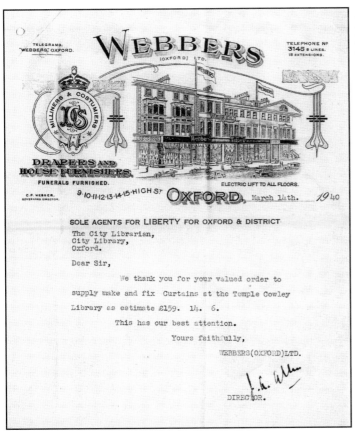

The children's department at Webbers where school uniforms, amongst other things, could be purchased.

More pictures from Webbers department store, above, ladies fashions, below, household goods. The pictures are believed to be taken in the late 1940s or early 1950s.

J Sainsbury's opened this shop at the top end of the High Street in 1911. Next door is Gill and Co., ironmongers, note the lawn mowers parked on the pavement. In 1927 they moved across the road and Sainsbury's took the opportunity to expand their shop. Sainsbury's closed their shop in 1974 when they moved into the Westgate Shopping Centre.

Also taken around 1950, these pictures show the meat, cheese and grocery counters, customers had to join the individual queues and at this time, would have still be using rationing coupons for some goods. The shop was beautifully decorated with ornate tiles on the floors and walls.

Sainsbury's vacated premises shortly after it closed in 1974.

This picture taken in about 1950, shows the pay desk which was sited at the rear of the store.

The High Street South side, from Rose Lane

No 68 Philips - the pen shop, this shop was still in business in 2008.

No 70 Oxford Health Food Stores

No 71 Eastgate Gallery - antique china

No 73 Eastgate Hotel

Oxford University Examination School

No 81-84 Frank Cooper's - "The Oxford Marmalade Shop". Frank Cooper's marmalade is one of Oxfords most celebrated products. Frank Cooper's marmalade was first produced in 1840 behind the High Street shop, made by Frank Cooper's wife Sarah for the Oxford students. In 1874 they opened a factory in Victoria Buildings on the Botley Road near the railway station. Frank Cooper's Ltd was taken over by Brown and Polson Ltd. The famous Frank Cooper's marmalade is no longer made in Oxford, although it is still available to buy from most supermarkets. The High Street shop closed and was taken over by the Co-op and was made into a high class restaurant, The Angel, which also catered for wedding receptions. It is now called The Grand Café - see photograph in chapter 4. The small building before The Grand Café is used by the Oxford Bus Company for their staff as a restroom and offices.

No 104 Sanders of Oxford Ltd - antiquarian books and prints, still trading in 2008.

No 108 Savory & Moore Ltd - a chemist on the corner of King Edward Street. The premises are now occupied by Oddbins UK Ltd, wine merchants.

No 109-113 Shepherd & Woodward Ltd - men's tailors, robe makers, sports and boys outfitters, also a men's hairdressers. This firm was started in Cornmarket Street in the 1800s by Arthur Shepherd, but moved to 110 High Street in the early 1920s, after merging with Woodward. This business is still trading and very popular with the University students for the hire of robes and gowns for their graduation ceremonies.

No 114 Hector Powell Ltd - men's tailors.

No 115 Rowell & Son Ltd - watch maker and jewellers. This shop moved to nearby Turl Street where it is still in business.

No 116 Oxford University Press Book Shop - the retail premises of the Oxford University Press in Walton Street.

No 119 Hall Bros Ltd - tailors established 1689, this shop is now Ede and Ravenscroft, men's tailors and still in business

No 124 Russell Acott Ltd - this shop sold televisions, radios and musical instruments also records and sheet music. The premises are now a coffee bar called All Bar One. Note the recent photograph I have taken showing the well worn tiled entrance into Russell Acott's (see page 32) and, looking up, see the decorations of cherubs with trumpets carved in the wood at the top of the window.

No 125 Castle & Co Ltd - wine and spirit merchants

No 126 Kendall & Sons Ltd - umbrella makers

No 127-128 True Form - shoe shop

No 128 Gill & Co - ironmongers. This ironmongers shop sold "everything" - saucepans, kettles, paint, nails and screws. These latter items were not sold in the large packets as they are available nowadays, but you could buy half a dozen or less as required. Also available were a variety of tools for use in the home, and mowers and seeds for the garden. Before I married in 1949 I bought a set of three Swan aluminum saucepans and, after nearly fifty years in use, I replaced them with stainless steal saucepans, a lot lighter to use and easier to clean. As we go to press it has been announced that Gills are to close after trading for 480 years. Are we doomed to live in a retail world of bland chain shops and warehouses?

No 131 Payne & Sons - goldsmiths and silversmiths. This is an old family business which started with a branch in Wallingford in approximately 1790. In 1889 George Septimus Payne opened the Oxford shop at 131 High Street. This business is still being run by Judy Payne, daughter of Edward Peter Payne, the seventh generation to own the Oxford shop. Judy has worked here since 1969 and became a director in 1979. She is the great granddaughter of George Septimus Payne, whose two grandsons are also retired directors. Still a family firm, in business for two centuries, and a lovely shop to visit. Please note the carved mastiff holding a clock above the shop frontage.

No 132 Belfast Linen Warehouse Ltd - linen and household items

No 133 Will R Rose Ltd - photography shop

No 134 Whites Cocktail Bar - very popular with the American service men to meet the local girls during the Second World War 1939-1945. Many Oxford girls became GI Brides and went to live in America.

No 135 Finlay & Co Ltd - tobacconist

No 136 Smarts Bros - furniture store

No 137 Savorys - tobacconist. Now Fellows of Oxford.

No 138 City of Oxford Motor Services Ltd - booking office for passenger transport

On the corner of High Street and St Aldates was Wyatts, an old fashioned haberdashery shop with a department selling babies viyella nightdresses, cherub vests and toweling nappies and children's liberty bodices. This is where I bought my baby clothes for my two daughters. No throw away nappies like today! This shop is now The Edinburgh Woollen Mill.

'The Oxford Marmalade' made famous by Frank Cooper who established his business in 1840.

The Angel Restaurant owned by the Co-op in 1945, previously Frank Cooper's premisses.

Hall Bros., Tailors, established in 1689, the premises are now occupies by Ede and Ravenscroft.

Russel Acott, sellers of tv's, radios, musical instruments, records and sheet music, In the days of records people would go and listen to their selection in one of the many small booths - and often as not leave without making a purchase! The shop closed in 1999.

Kendall & Sons Ltd specialised in umbrellas and mackintosh's. On the right hand side can be seen the entrance to The Vincent Printing works and Baxter's Press.

Next to Kendall & Sons was Gill & Co., having moved from its previous premises next to Sainsbury's just opposite. Gills relocated again into Wheatsheaf Yard, where they still are today.

Belfast Linen Warehouse Ltd in 1921. Next door was Will R Rose Ltd who sold photographic equipment. On the right of Will R. Rose is the entrance to Whites Bar which was very popular with the young.

On the corner of High Street and St Aldates was Wyatts, an old fashioned haberdashery shop, now the premises of Edinburgh Woollen Mill.

CHAPTER 5

Queen Street

Queen Street, South side, from St Aldates to Castle Street

No 4 Freeman Hardy & Willis Ltd - shoe shop

No 5 Paige - ladies fashion

No 6 Reed & Sons Ltd - tailors also specialists in boys' school uniform

No 7 Kirners Bros - jewellers established in 1864

No 9 John Lane Menswear - tailors and outfitters

No 10 Maypole Dairy Co Ltd – grocers

No 11 John Plant Ltd - shoe shop

No 12 Lotus & Delta Ltd - boot maker

No 13-17 Badcocks - departmental shop. A wonderful shop - see chapter 2 for my memories of this shop. The photograph shows the driver of Badcocks van, Alfred Alder. When Badcocks closed, the premises were acquired by the Oxford Co-operative.

In March 1978 Marks & Spencer's exchanged premises with the Oxford Co-op moving from their large shop in Cornmarket Street opposite the Cadena Café. Marks & Spencer's are still in business in Queen Street, unfortunately the lovely frontage of Badcocks was demolished with the building of the new Marks & Spencer's. Next door to Badcocks was the ABC Electra cinema - see photograph opposite. When the Oxford Co-op acquired Badcocks the cinema was combined to make larger premises.

No 18 Halfords Cycle Co Ltd - cycle maker

No 19 Hepworths Ltd - tailors

No 22 Tylers Ltd - shoe shop. Note the style of shoes as shown in the photographs of Tylers.

Daveys, Singers and Bakers – these shops were all demolished to make way for a large new building, the City Chambers, offices for the Oxford City Council. This site is now the BHS Store.

Badcocks department store, the ABC Electra Cinema was next door.

The material counter in Badcocks where customers could sit while choosing their purchase..

Badcocks van driver, Alfred Alder.

Oxford Co-op acquired these premises from Badcocks, now Marks & Spencer.

At the bottom of Queen Street and the corner of St Ebbes, these shops were demolished in 1959 to make way for the new City Chambers, the offices of the City Council. The building was later redeveloped and is now BHS (formerly known as British Home Stores).

Tylers, another Queen Street shop, a window display of elegant shoes.

Queen Street, North side, from Carfax

No 45 Ballard Ltd – jewellers and silversmiths. This shop is now Crabtree and Evelyn which sells soaps, hand creams and specialist gifts particularly for the festive season.

No 44 Lipton Ltd - grocery shop. Note the window display and prices of items for sale shown in pounds, shillings and pence before the introduction of decimal currency. Also note the frontage of the windows proudly proclaiming "Purveyors of Tea to the late King George."

This photograph shows the demolition of number 41, Timothy Whites & Taylor the chemist, and number 39, Oxford and District Co-operative, confectioners, café and dairy. These buildings were demolished in 1984 to provide the entrance into a new shopping arcade, the Clarendon Centre, which extends through to the other entrance in Cornmarket Street, with an exit via Shoe Lane into New Inn Hall Street.

No 38 Barratts Shoes. This shop is still in business. Above Barratts Shoe Shop was Harrisons, ladies and gents hairdresser which moved to premises above Mac Fisheries in Castle Street, which was demolished in 1969 when the Westgate Shopping Centre was built. Two more old Oxford businesses closed.

No 36-37 John Collier - tailors. This shop was known as Fifty Shilling Tailors. Crawfords Cafeteria was above John Collier. This restaurant was a popular eating place, enjoyed by young and old, a place to meet up with friends to enjoy a coffee or lunch. Crawfords was originally the Wilberforce Hotel. Note the original frontage above John Collier showing the architecture of this building. Most of the buildings have retained their original frontage on this side of Queen Street, except where two buildings were demolished to make way for the new entrance to the Clarendon Centre.

No 35 Milletts & Co Ltd - outfitters. This shop is still in business but has moved to 42 Queen Street near Carfax

No 33 W Timpson Ltd - shoe shop

No 32 A Bennett Ltd - ladies clothes

No 31 Crown Wallpapers - this was such an interesting shop but forced to close when the large superstores started trading in wallpaper and paints.

No 30 Currys Ltd - electrical goods and cycle shop. A picture, with what is by todays standards, a very large number of staff, can be seen on page 47. This shop relocated to the Botley Road.

No 28 Alkit Ltd - tailors

No 27 Freeman Hardy & Willis Ltd - shoe shop, these premises are now a jewellers, on the corner with New Inn Hall Street.

In 1966 there were 8 shoe shops and two jewellers in Queen Street.

Adjacent to the Carfax Tower, these premises were occupied by jewellers Ballards until around 1982. The premises were then occupied by Crabtree and Evelyn.

Lipton's window display offers the sound advice to 'spend your points wisely', an obvious reference to war time (or just post war) food rationing.

Timothy White & Taylor and the Co-op premises were demolished in 1984 to make way for the entrance to the new Clarendon Shopping Centre.

Barratts shoe shop, above was ladies and gents hairdresser, Harrison's.

Sometimes called the 'fifty shilling tailor', John Collier was, as the slogan says, 'the window to watch'. Above, was Crawfords Caféteria, its popularity cannot be under-stated. the premises were previously occupied by the Wilberforce Hotel.

A broad view of the north side of Queen Street.

Looking down Queen Street, the building in view at the junction of Castle Street and New Road was occupied by fishmonger, Mac Fisheries. It was demolished in 1969.

Assembled outside Currys Queen Street shop is more than two dozen staff! How times change! However, as can be seen Currys were selling more than electrical appliances.

Freeman, Hardy & Willis, shoe shop situated on the corner of Queen Street and New Inn Hall Street. The premises are now occupied by Beaverbrooks, Jeweller's.

CHAPTER 6

Castle Street

At the bottom end of Queen Street, on the south side past St Ebbes Street, the following photographs show these five shops before they were demolished in 1969 to make way for the new shopping centre, the Westgate Centre, also the new Oxford Central Library, which relocated from St Aldates.

G R Cooper – ironmongers. This large department store was situated on the corner of Castle Street and St Ebbes, at the end of Queen Street. The building was built in art deco style, but unfortunately the façade was lost when the building was demolished.

Next to G R Cooper was number 4 Halifax House with Halifax Building Society, above which were the offices of Challenor & Son and Gardiner, solicitors, which are still in business in Oxford.

No 5 Butlers & Co Ltd - bakers and grocery shop

No 7, 10 and 11 Starlings Oxford Ltd. This shop specialized in floor covering, good quality carpets, including those manufactured by Wilton and Axminster. In the 1940s and 50s it was more usual to have a square carpet in the middle of the room, with either lino or stained floorboards around the outside. Starlings had an excellent rage of linoleum (lino), a popular, and cheaper, alternative to carpet, sometimes with a rug laid next to the fire. Starlings employed staff to make curtains from their stock of material to customers' requirements, also to fit carpets.

No 12 Paviers Arms Public House

On the corner of Castle Street and New Road was Mac Fisheries, a wet fish shop selling all kinds of fish, cod, haddock and plaice also kippers and herrings. See chapter 3 for my memories of this shop.

All these shops and buildings were demolished to make way for the new Westgate Shopping Centre, and the Oxford Central Library. Another part of Oxford I remember that has changed beyond recognition.

G R Cooper, ironmongers and builders merchants were established in the 19th century. This building was built in the art deco style, many will remember the sprung wooden floors within. Acquired by Selfridges in 1966 but demolished in 1969 to make way for the new Westgate development.

Many will remember looking inside Mac Fisheries to see the fish tank set into the floor. In the picture on page 46 the building can be seen at the junction of Castle Street and New Road (formerly Main Road).

This view taken from New Road shows the fencing surrounding the site where Mac Fisheries stood.

Selfridges new store in the Westgate Shopping Centre.

At the top end of Castle Street was Starlings carpet shop and the Paviers' Arms public house.

CHAPTER 7

St Ebbes Street

This small street was a great place to explore with its quaint old fashioned shops.

West side

No 39 G R Cooper (Oxford) Ltd. From the top of Queens Street, this large department store extended into St Ebbes.

No 37 G R Cooper (Oxford) Ltd - this was the electrical department.

No 35-36 Peter Richards of Oxford Ltd - ladies fashions

No 33 Broadribb Ltd - cycle dealers

No 28-32 F Cape & Co Ltd - established 1887 - drapers, haberdashery, furniture, outfitters and boots and shoes. In February 1972 this well known Oxford drapery store closed down after nearly a hundred years of business. In December 1971 Capes had its last sale before closing down. I am dedicating this book to the memory of my late mother-in-law Doris Eva Bleay, who worked at Capes and had very happy memories of her time there. This was also a favourite shop of mine which I have written about in chapter 3. When F Cape & Co was demolished a new building was built and Fenwicks opened a new store, ladies clothes and a hairdressing department, very up market. It was a large shop and had another entrance near the back of the Westgate Shopping Centre where the new Sainsbury's moved to from High Street.

Just past St Ebbes Church was number 26-27 PE Davis Ltd - furniture dealers. This was an old fashioned furniture shop and was run by two brothers.

Perrings - the furniture shop in George Street which moved into a new building on the corner of Church Street. These premises have now been converted into a gymnasium, with offices on the first floor.

East side

No 1 Davey Bros - home furnishers

No 2 Singer Sewing Machine Co Ltd

No 3 G T Jones & Co Ltd - wine and spirit merchants

No 4 Shirley Smith of Oxford Ltd - dry cleaners

No 5 Radio Rentals Ltd - radio and television rental company

No 6 Chiltern Dry Cleaners

No 7 Ivor Fields Ltd - photographers

No 9-10 Peter Richards of Oxford - fashion wear

No 11 F Cape & Co Ltd - men's and boys' outfitters

No 12 Oxonian Travel Services Ltd

No 13 The Royal Blenheim Public House, corner of Pembroke Street.

On the opposite corner was another old fashion drapery store, the St Ebbes Cash Drapery Stores, known as SPQR. My mother used to work here before she married.

F. Cape & Co. established in 1887, closed in 1972. Their business was run from a number of premises in St. Ebbes, each shop specialising in different goods. Although 'old fashioned', it was well loved.

The closing down sale.

Two more pictures from Cape's, the haberdashery counter, note the bentwood chair where weary customers can rest. The counter and shelves were saved and are on view at the Oxford Museum .

Another pair of Cape pictures, the lady is Mrs Wyn Goodey busy on her 'adding machine'. Sadly Wyn was looking forward to seeing this book but died before its publication.

Sited in one corner of the office is this wall clock advertising 'world renowned Fitu Corsets', no doubt supplied by the corset maker!

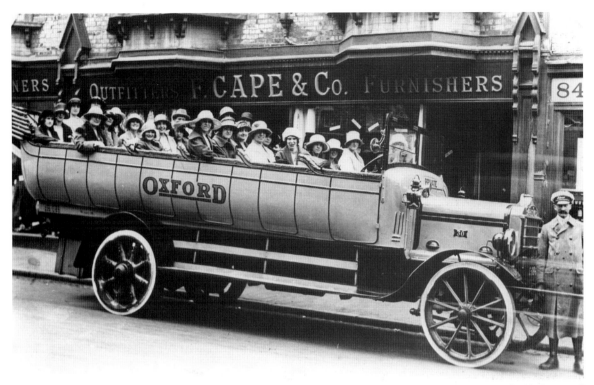

This final Cape's picture thought to date from 1926 shows the staff outside the Cowley Road shop about to embark on a works outing, Eva Blay, mother-in-law of the author can be seen sitting in the middle of the back row, (Eva Blay married Fred Bleay in July, 1936).

This letterhead of St Ebbes Cash Drapery Stores gives a clue to the huge range of goods sold. The drawing of the premises shows the letters SPQR over what looks like a doorway at the corner of the building. Evidently it stood for 'small profits quick return'.

P E Davies, another St Ebbes furniture shop was run by two brothers, sadly another demolished building.

The Bijou Stores, a grocery shop in Commercial Road, St Ebbes, was run by Mr & Mrs Rogers. Mr Rogers taught banjo, mandolin and guitar in his studio - a small sign can be seen to the left and just above the door. Their son, Stan Rogers achieved fame playing music with the 'Blue Stars Players'.

CHAPTER 8

Cornmarket Street and Market Street

Cornmarket Street East side

Lloyds Bank, on the corner of Cornmarket Street and High Street.

No 2 Margetts for Hats. Hats were popular for men, especially bowler hats for business men, also caps and trilbys. When Margetts closed this shop was occupied by Watches of Switzerland Ltd - watch specialists.

No 3 Geo E Weeks & Co - the city restaurant and confectioner's who had their bakery, the Swan Bakery, in Paradise Street, St Thomas's. This bakery was opposite St Georges tower by Quaking Bridge. The restaurant premises were later occupied by J Lyons & Co Ltd - a very popular café, served by waitresses who were fondly called Nippys.

No 4 Freeman Hardy & Willis Ltd - shoe shop

No 5 Golden Cross Hotel

No 6 Dorothy Perkins Ltd - lingerie

No 7 Dunn & Co Ltd - hatters

No 8 Boots Ltd – chemist. In 1957 F W Woolworths Ltd and H Samuel Ltd Jewellers moved to new premises, the Clarendon Centre, on the opposite side of Cornmarket. Boots the chemist enlarged their premises by taking over the vacant buildings and opened their new large shop in time for Christmas 1957. Boots are still trading on this site and have kept most of the old façade above the ground floor.

The photograph of F W Woolworth Ltd at the end of this chapter shows the jubilee celebrations in 1935.

No 9-10 H Samuel Ltd - jewellers

No 9-10 Maison Gay - ladies hairdresser above Samuels

No 11-12 Noel Fashions Ltd - ladies fashions

This view taken from Carfax and looking down Cornmarket Street, shows Margetts, a men's hat shop. Literally any kind of hat for working men and business men could be purchased.

Looking towards Carfax, on the left can be seen Geo E Weeks & Co, a restaurant and cake shop. Established in 1911 it closed around 1956.

F W Woolworth was established in 1925, the flags were put up to celebrate the Silver Jubilee of King George V in 1935. On Woolworth's shop sign you can read '3d and 6d stores', a reference to their early marketing strategy.

H. Samuel, moved opposite side to the Clarendon Centre in 1957. Above Samuels's was ladies hairdresser, Maison Gay.

Market Street South side - from Cornmarket Street to Turl Street.

Mac Fisheries Ltd - fishmongers. This shop moved to Market Street when their other shop in Castle Street was demolished to make way for the Westgate shopping centre and library.

Mothercare Ltd. This shop sold baby clothes, prams and cots, also high chairs. When this shop closed, Mothercare moved to the Cowley retail park, near the large supermarket Tescos, and are still in business.

C H Brown & Son were also in Market Street. They are an old established business selling leather goods, including saddles, harness and dog requisites. When this shop closed they moved into the covered market and are still in business.

These shops on this side of this street were demolished when Boots the chemist acquired the old premises of Woolworths in Cornmarket Street to enlarge their shop and make an exit into Market Street.

Market Street North side - from Cornmarket Street to Turl Street

Arthur Rowles Ltd - seeds man and florist

Wenborn - selling knives and scissors

Strange (Oxford) Ltd - hairdresser. There were two shops belonging to Mr W Strange on either side of the road. On the south side was the men's hairdressers and on the north side was the ladies. When these shops were demolished Mr Strange moved to the end of Market Street near Turl Street.

All these shops were demolished to enlarge the premises of Marks & Spencers in Cornmarket and provide a pedestrian exit into Market Street.

C H Brown & Son, dealt in quality leather goods and was an early Market Street trader. The shop premises below was demolished to make way for Marks & Spencer's enlarged shop on the corner of Cornmarket and Market Street. Browns are still trading in the Covered Market.

Another early picture, Arthur Rowles, Seedsman and Florist.

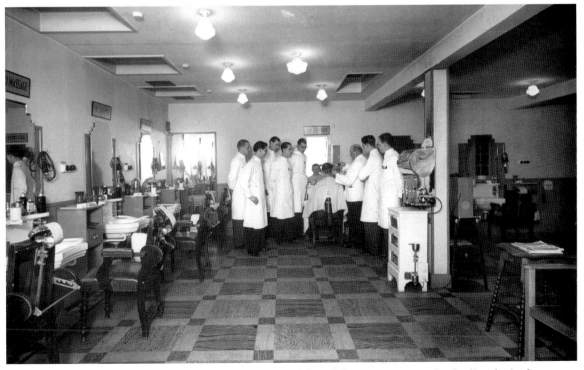

Men's hairdresser, Strange, on the opposite side of the street was the ladies hair dresser.

Cornmarket Street East side

No 13-20 Marks & Spencers Ltd. This department store was situated in Cornmarket Street until March 1978 when they moved to Queen Street, after exchanging premises with the Oxford Co-operative.

When the Oxford Co-op opened their new shop in Cornmarket the first and ground floors sold clothes, china and furniture, and in the large basement was a large grocery department selling fresh vegetables also meat, cheese, etc. This grocery department was used by local people, also students and people in their lunch break.

No 21 Milward & Sons Ltd - shoe shop. This shop supplied ladies, men's and children's shoes, in well known brands including Clarks, Brevitts and Startrite children's shoes and sandals. In those days the assistants always measured the children's feet to ensure a perfect fit. Milwards was demolished in 1962 to make way for the expansion of the Marks & Spencers store.

No 22 W H Smith & Sons Ltd. This shop is still in business in Cornmarket selling newspapers and books.

No 23 Green's Costumiers

No 24 Fullers Ltd - restaurant and cake shop. This was a very nice restaurant and the cake shop sold a large variety of cakes, I especially liked the large coffee sandwich cake with chopped walnuts and coffee cream filling and coffee icing on the top, decorated with whole walnuts, it was delicious. The photograph of Fullers was taken in 1922.

No 26 Lambert - shoe shop.

No 27 Zacharias & Co. This was an old established shop, known as "Zacs for Macs" in their advertisements promoting their waterproof garments as their specialty was mackintosh raincoats for ladies and gentlemen. I remember in the early 1950s I bought myself a beige ladies trench style raincoat. It was certainly waterproof and very fashionable at that time. I went to Thame show this year and you can still buy this style of raincoat which is very popular with the horsey set and country pursuit people. Zacharias's shop was originally occupied by Harvey & Company, tea dealers during the late nineteenth and early twentieth century. This historic building with its half timber frontage is one of the most interesting buildings in Cornmarket Street, and I hope it will never be demolished.

No 28 Speedwell Cleaning Co 1950 Ltd - dyers and cleaners

No 30 Bollom Ltd - dyers and cleaners

No 31 Oxford Drug Company Ltd - chemist, also providing the entrance to Boswells toy shop. The Oxford Drug Co merged with Boswell's Ltd, and the premises has two entrances, one from Cornmarket Street and the other entrance from Broad Street.

Marks & Spencer, boys department.

The food department was housed in the basement. In March 1978 Marks & Spencer exchanged premises with the Co-op Store which was situated in Queen Street.

Cornmarket Street shoe shop, Milwards employed a large number of staff.

Fuller's restaurant and cake shop was established in 1921 and closed in 1972. Next door was Lambert's shoe shop.

Jimmy Dingle walking up Cornmarket Street, His advertising board inviting people to attend an 'Ideal Home and Trades Exhibition' at the Town Hall, Jimmy was known and respected by most residents of Oxford.

One of the more interesting buildings in Cornmarket Street was the premises of Zacharias, established in 1850. Zacharias were famous for their trench style raincoats for both ladies and gentlemen. Their slogan 'Zacs for Macs' (can be seen on the previous page) was emblazoned on Oxford buses for many years. Zacharias closed in 1976.

Cornmarket Street, West side - from Carfax

No 65 Midland Bank Ltd. This is now HSBC Bank.

No 63 Carfax Assembly Rooms. These premises were owned by the Oxford and District Co-operative Society Ltd. This building was used for ballroom dancing and in the entrance to the Assembly rooms there was a small shop which sold cigarettes and cigars. When this building closed it was amalgamated with the HSBC Bank.

No 61 Montague Burton Ltd - men's tailors. This shop is now Moss Bros.

Crown Yard and the Crown Inn

No 56-58 Grimbly Hughes & Co Ltd, established in 1840. This was a high class grocery and wine shop. The premises are now McDonalds, a favourite place for young children to visit for burger and chips, also with the foreign students and visitors. The original frontage above the burger shop is still there.

No 53-52 F W Woolworth & Co Ltd. This new shop was built on the site of the Clarendon Hotel, after moving from their old shop on the opposite side of Cornmarket in 1957. Sadly this large store closed on 29 January 1983. The two photographs at the end of this chapter show Viola Hancock who was chief cashier at the time of closure, also Roy Rudman of Woolworths maintenance team with the flag flying at half mast to mark the sad occasion of the closure of this store. The Clarendon Hotel was used in the Second World War 1939-1945 for injured soldiers. It was demolished to make way for the new shopping centre to be built, named the Clarendon Centre after the hotel.

No 51 Scotch Wool & Hosiery Stores. This shop sold knitting wool, and wool and canvas to make rugs which were very popular in those days, being a most rewarding hobby. This lovely gothic style building built approximately in the 1880s is still in existence. The shop was originally a men's tailors and robe makers owned by Arthur Woodward and Mr Richmond until the early 1920s when the business moved to 110 High Street after amalgamating with Mr Shepherd. This business is still trading in the High Street as Shepherd and Woodward Ltd.

No 50 Boynton. Above Boynton's was Godfrey Court hairdresser.

No 48 Sands - milliners. This was a hat shop for ladies, most people used to wear hats in the old days, especially to church.

No 47-44 Cadena Café Ltd. This was a lovely cake and bread shop, also a smart restaurant and coffee specialist. I have written about the Cadena in chapter 3 recalling my memories of my favourite shops. The new shop to replace the Cadena was a haberdashery and material shop called Gordon Thody Fabrics. This shop closed and now it is HMV selling videos and CDs.

If you look up above the shop fronts in Cornmarket, High Street and part of Queen Street you will see that most of the architecture has been retained. In my younger days I never appreciated the design and architecture of buildings but since writing this book it has opened my eyes and interest of the beautiful old buildings of this city where I was born.

No 43 Mansfield & Sons - shoe shop

No 41-42 A L Salisbury Ltd - leather goods

No 40 F Blagrove & Co - opticians, established 1865.

No 39 Austin Reed Ltd - men's and ladies outfitters. This building was originally the Plough Inn; note the sign also the old building in the photographs at the end of this chapter.

St Michael's Street

No 37 Royal Insurance Group

No 36 Northgate Tavern

No 35 Oxford & District Co-op - jewellers and boys' sport outfitters

No 34-33 Dolcis Shoe Co - ladies, men's and children's shoes

No 32 National Provincial Bank

A view of Carfax Tower with the Midland Bank on the corner of Cornmarket Street.

Grimbly Hughes & Co., were established in 1840 and closed in 1958. They were a re-nowned supplier of groceries, cooked meats and wines, both wholesale and retail. Grimbly Hughes might be gone but the splendid architecture can still be seen above Macdonald's.

The abundant display of goods on sale at Grimbly and Hughes.

Looking down Cornmarket Street can be seen the Clarendon Hotel. It closed in 1954 and eventually became the part of the site for the new Woolworth store and the Clarendon Shopping Centre. Below is one of the drawings for the new store which was to be relatively short lived.

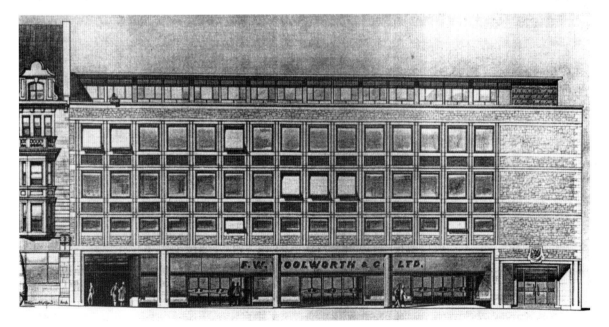

Roy Rudman seen saluting the Woolworth flag flying at half mast at the
closure of the store.

Chief cashier Viola Hancock at the
moment of closure, 4pm, 29th January 1983.

Moving further down Cornmarket Street brings the Cadena Café into view, This was a wonderful place to take afternoon tea with cream cakes, complete with pinafored waitress service. It was also noted for the amazing aroma of coffee which would find its way on to the street. Upstairs was a restaurant which catered for wedding receptions. Established in the 1920s, closed in 1970s and the building demolished. Of all the shops that Oxford has lost this is possibly the one still talked about the most.

The ground floor of the Cadena café.

Jimmy Dingle and his bride celebrate their wedding in the first floor restaurant in 1950.
Marks & Spencer shop sign can be seen out of the window and across the road.

A hand written bill from 1941 for coffee, tea, bread and biscuits for the grand sum of 9/2½d, about 46 pence!

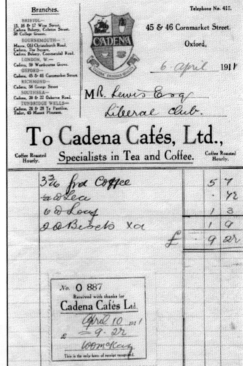

The Scotch Wool & Hosery Stores, Boyntons and Sands, the frontages of these shops still remain.

Moving down Cornmarket Street, is Manfield & Sons, further down on the corner of St Michael's Street is Austin Read which was formally the Plough Inn, The shop sign above the door incorporates the figure of a plough.

CHAPTER 9

George Street and a short history of Hill Upton and Co Ltd

George Street has changed a lot since the 1950s; it is now all wine bars and restaurants. The shops that I remember the most have all disappeared.

Pleasance and Harper - jewellers and watch makers. This is where I purchased my engagement ring.

Twinings Bros - this was an old established high class grocer.

John Perrings - this was a good quality furniture shop.

Southern Electricity Showrooms. This business on the corner of George Street and New Inn Hall Street was opened in 1937. On the ground floor was the spacious showroom which displayed electric cookers, electric fires also washing machines and other small electrical appliances. On the ground floor was the accounts office where customers paid their electricity bill. The floors above were used for demonstration purposes, also offices for the management and staff.

Oxford and District Co-operative. This was a large building opposite the old Fire Station. The individual shops consisted of a butchers, a large grocery shop and a furniture shop where my late husband and I bought a well made dark oak bedroom suite. My grandson has in his possession the small gentleman's wardrobe, still in use today 60 years on. There was also a large drapery and millinery shop. The Oxford and District Co-op had their offices above this large building where you took your "divi" share book to be made up every year. When you joined the Co-op you became a share holder member, with your own personal number and when you bought items from the Co-op shops you were given a ticket when asked for your number, and this was a good way to save money. This building with its lovely façade is still in George Street but the premises are no longer being used by the Oxford Co-op. See the frontage of this building in the photograph at the end of this chapter.

Normans Ladies Fashions. This small shop sold ladies underwear and I bought my trousseau for my wedding in 1949 with the remainder of the clothing coupons I had saved. I bought a pure silk dressing gown also a night dress to match. It was expensive but I used them for a long time, they were very good quality

George Street, South side

St George's Mansion. On the corner of Cornmarket Street and George Street, this imposing building with the green dome was once the home of the George Hotel and the National Provincial Bank. The hotel closed in 1911 but the George Restaurant continued and was considered one of the city's best restaurants to visit. Although the picture on page 86 shows the building in all its glory, the imposing dome can also be seen in the photographs of the Clarendon Hotel and the Cadena Café on the west side of Cornmarket Street. The building is now home to the Natwest Bank.

No 1 Alliance Building Society

No 3 Pleasance and Harper - jewellers and watch makers, now closed. Other premises above number 3 included Del-Nevo ladies hairdresser. Mr Francis Del-Nevo was brother of Mr Angelo Del-Nevo who was also a ladies hairdresser in High Street near to Leslie Davey and West, the jewellers, where I worked for two years. Also in premises above number 3 was a dentist, Sharpes.

No 5 Rose's Fashions Ltd - ladies clothes

No 7 The Grapes Public House, which is still in existence. This has a lovely façade which you can see in the photograph at the end of this chapter.

No 9-13 John Perrings Ltd - house furnishers. This shop moved to new premises in St Ebbes, but the business has now closed.

No 15-19 Twinings Bros Ltd. This was a high class grocery shop also a tobacconist and wine store, but now closed. Twinings also owned a grocery shop at 294 Banbury Road.

No 21 Wilsons - ladies fashions

No 23 H & A Conway Ltd - opticians

No 25 Sketchley Cleaners Ltd - dry cleaning

No 27 Eveline Lambert - shoe shop

No 29-31 City Motor Co (Oxford) Ltd. This was the show room for Vauxhall cars.

No 33-35 Hill Upton and Co Ltd. This was an old established business which started trading in Oxford in May 1890 at various premises until they moved to larger premises in George Street in August 1925.

Hill Upton and Co Ltd

The business of Hill Upton and Co was established in Oxford in May 1890 as a branch of Hill Lawrence and Hooper of Millbank Street, Westminster, London. A showroom and office was opened on the first floor of the premises of William Baker and Co at Broad Street, Oxford. Shortly after the opening of this branch the business was carried on by Mr Edmund L Hill, a grandson of Sir Rowland Hill, the famous pioneer of Penny Postage, under the title of Hill and Co. The business was transferred to rooms in New Inn Hall Street (now St Michaels Street) over the premises of Steane and Co and later on moved to Magdalen Street at the corner of Friars Entry, where James Powell and Sons, the Whitefriars Glass Works formerly had showrooms. The title Hill Upton and Co dates from this move, when Mr W T Upton became a partner in the firm in 1903.

In 1925 larger premises became necessary and the new site was obtained in George Street where modern up to date buildings known as Radiant House were designed by Mr J R Wilkins for Mr W T Upton and Mr H J Butterfield and built by Wooldridge and Simpson. On the top of the roof of this building are two lanterns made of concrete, these are replicas of the original lanterns made by Wooldridge and Simpson on show at the British Exhibition to commemorate the year 1925 when Hill Upton's Radiant House was built.

Since the retirement of Mr W T Upton, the business of Hill Upton and Co has been carried on under the proprietorship of Mr H J Butterfield who had been the managing partner since 1913. Sadly the late Alderman Frederick Butterfield of Hill End Farm of Eynsham Road, Botley died December 1920 age 73 years, he had four sons and one daughter, and he was a veteran member of the city council. The Butterfield family ran Hill Upton and Co as a family business until this was taken over by F G Aldens, an Oxford company.

Hill Uptons were a well known and prestigious company and carried out electrical work at various premises including installing electric lighting at Elliston and Cavell in Magdalen Street also William Baker in Broad Street and Christchurch College in St Aldates also New College and schools including Mathew Arnold School. In 1935 they did the installation of permanent artificial lighting in the Sheldonian Theatre in Broad Street also in the Bodleian Library. Hill Uptons were the registered Electrical Contractors to the War Office also the Principal Colleges of Oxford and the Oxford Corporation.

Hill Uptons offered a wide range of goods and appliances including Hoover cleaners, Bendix washing machines and Kenwood Chef food mixers which are still available today, see the picture on page 91 advertising demonstrations.

In 1972 the firm Darke and Taylor who have premises in Kidlington took over from F G Alden. Mr David Newton who worked for F G Alden and Mr John Darke became partners and David Newton's son, Simon Newton, is also working for this electrical firm, the second generation still run as a family business.

When I started writing this book about the old shops of Oxford that have disappeared, my friend Simon Newton and his father David Newton of Darke and Taylor inherited lots of old photographs and books and papers of Hill Upton's history from F G Aldens, the previous owners and asked me if I would like them to include in my book. I really appreciate their generosity and permission to include the old photographs and the history of this old established firm. The remaining photographs and papers were donated by David and Simon Newton to the Oxfordshire photographic archive department of the central library in the Westgate.

No 37 Southern Electricity Board. On the corner of New Inn Hall Street.

No 39 Timms Stores - toy shop

No 45 Jane's Tuck Shop and Post Office

No 59-69 Oxford & District Co-operative - shops and offices

No 71 H Beechey - stationer's

No 71 Normans - ladies fashions

No 73 Oliver & Son (Oxford) Ltd - printers

No 75 Speedy Shoe Repairs

No 77-79 Ilco Ltd - electrical and refrigeration engineers

George Street, North side

No 3 Elliston and Cavell Ltd. A large shop which had lots of different departments selling many kinds of goods.

No 6   Lavalette Ltd - ladies fashions

No 8   Parslows of Reading Ltd - bakers

No 10 Melson Wingate Ltd - opticians

No 14 Colebrook - fishmonger. Note the photograph at the end of this chapter, showing a display of herring.

No 16 Clarendon Restaurant

Victoria Court and the New Theatre

No 24-26 Oxford & District Co-operative - hardware store

Gloucester Street, Three Ways House, The Arcade. This large building belonged to the Oxford & District Co-operative and there were a large selection of shops, including a chemist, opticians, confectioners, greengrocer and florist, also an electrical shop selling toasters, kettles, food mixers and televisions. At the front of Three Ways House was a milk bar which was a very popular venue for teenagers to meet for milkshakes and snacks after a visit to the Ritz Cinema.

No 36 Charles Geddes (Oxford) Ltd. This shop sold modern and antique furniture.

The Ritz Cinema

No 40 The Fire Station

No 44 Gardiners - opticians

No 46 Westwoods - radio and high-fidelity specialists

No 48 Welsh Pony Public House

No 50 Municipal Restaurant, serving a very reasonably priced meals. This was popular with students and people who worked in Oxford.

On the corner of Cornmarket Street and George Street stands St George's Mansion, originally home of the George Hotel which closed in 1911. Above the corner door you can see the sign for the George Restaurant which was on the second floor. At the time this picture was taken it was occupied by the National Provincial Bank, later Natwest Bank.

The Grapes public house in George Street, has been here for a long time and is still very popular, particularly with theater goers as it stands opposite the New Theatre.

John Perring Ltd., established in 1895 in George Street, they sold house furnishings. Another Oxford shop that was to relocate to new premises. In 1976 they moved to the new Westgate shopping centre in St Ebbes.

Twining Brothers window displays from 1940. The display celebrates 100 years of trade with New Zealand. The notice in the bottom right hand corner appears to confirm the display is a winner in a Daily Mail contest. The picture on the next page shows a display filled with eggs from Australia, these pictures are a reminder of a time when trade with Commonwealth countries was at its height.

Hill Upton & Co., was established in 1890, in 1925 larger premises were built and named Radiant House, note the two concrete lanterns on the roof.

This street scene shows electric light bulbs being delivered by horse and cart.

Alderman Frederick Butterfield, Managing Partner from 1913.

Kenwood food mixers were once a much desired kitchen accessory.

The staff take their places for this photograph taken in 1925.

Colebrook fishmongers and their display of fresh fish.

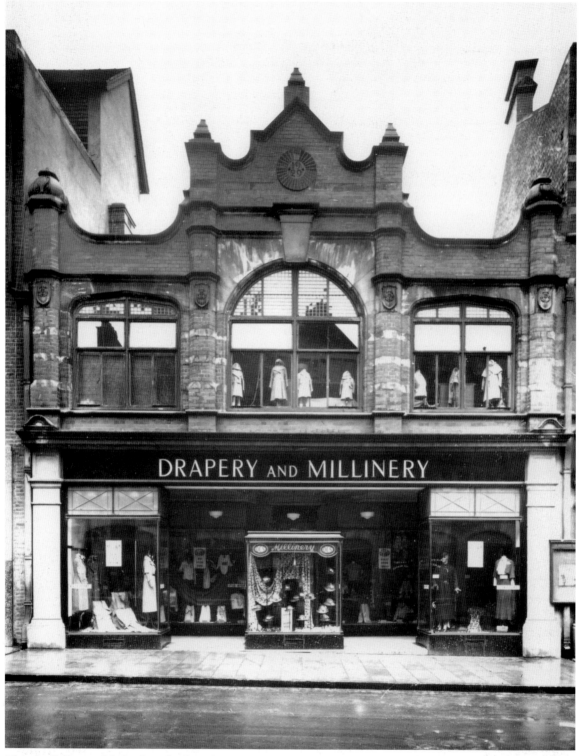

This building with its lovely façade opposite the old fire station is no longer being used by the Co-op.

Demolition of Three Way House in George Street, owned by Oxford Co-op. Sadly this brought about the closure of Charles Geddes, a quality furniture shop.

At the bottom end of George Street on the corner of Worcester Street was Ilco, retailer of electrical goods and services.

CHAPTER 10

Magdalen Street and Broad Street

Magdalen Street, from Cornmarket to St Giles

No 3 Charles Taphouse & Son Ltd. This shop sold radios, record players, pianos and other musical instruments. Customers could listen to records in small listening booths before deciding which records to purchase. My late husband, before we were married, used to spend a lot of time at this shop when he came home on leave from the army, as he loved all the popular songs and classical music. Sid's mother bought a small radiogram for our wedding present so we could both enjoy the music. We also had an HMV (His Masters Voice) portable wind up gramophone which we took on the river when we went on a punt up the river to visit the Victoria Arms public house in Old Marston. Taphouse closed in 1984.

No 4-12 Elliston and Cavell Ltd, established 1823. This was a large departmental store with a back entrance into Friars Entry. The shop had lots of departments selling furniture, household items and a good selection of kitchen and china in the basement also a toy department and, at Christmas, a grotto with a Father Christmas giving presents to the children. Also ladies and children's clothes and a department which altered clothes and made curtains from material bought from their furnishing department. This shop is now Debenhams.

Friars Entry
No 18 Super Cinema
No 19 Nurse The Furrier. Above Nurse was Rita Sloan Ltd - ladies hairdressers

Broad Street

On the corner of Cornmarket Street and Broad Street was William Baker Ltd. This shop sold furniture, china and glassware. It is now Waterstones Book Shop.

No 1-4 H Boswell & Co Ltd. This shop opened in 1738 selling luggage and household items. In 1880 the firm was taken over by the Pearson Family and is still a family owned business. Mr Jonathan Pearson, managing director, and Sarah, his cousin, are both on the board of directors. In 1929 the Oxford Drug Co and H Boswell and Son were merged. This shop is very popular with the Oxford students buying kitchen equipment to use when they live in rented property and do their own cooking. Above Boswell's was Bretts School of Dancing where the teenagers used to go to learn ballroom dancing. On the second floor was a small café called Kemps Cafeteria which was very popular with the teenagers to meet after their session at Bretts.

No 9-10 Howes Model Shop. This shop sold toys and model kits of every description. They stocked Meccano and Hornby train sets, and lots of accessories for making railway lay-outs. This was a popular shop for small boys and their dads, where they could browse and choose items to add to their train collection. My brother Michael was 12 years younger than me, and when I went to work I used to take him on my day off to choose small items to add to his Hornby train collection, which my father had bought him. Sadly another shop that has closed.

No 11 J Thornton & Son - new and secondhand bookseller. This was an old fashioned book shop, a favourite of mine to browse and often find an old book I had been looking for. Sadly this shop has closed, and it is now a café. Note in the photographs of Thorntons at the end of this chapter, the small photograph showing the much worn tiled step with the name of Thornton still visible.

No 12 R Gillman & Son - high class shop selling very expensive shoes.

No 13 Castell & Son Ltd - men's tailors and robe makers

No 14 Hunts Ltd - office equipment

No 15 Lloyds Bank

No 17 Oxfam. This was the first shop opened in Oxford for famine relief and also to raise funds for major disasters overseas.

No 18 Art & Stationery Co Ltd. This shop stocked artist materials and were picture frame makers.

No 19 G E Taylor - tailor and robe makers

No 20 West & Sons - florist. They also had a florist shop in the covered market off Market Street and their plant nursery and shop was in Windmill Road in Headington Oxford. Sadly the shop and nursery in Headington has been demolished and houses built on the site.

No 21 Millin & Co Ltd - furriers

No 22 The Children's Book Shop

No 23 The Paperback Shop

No 24-25 F A Wood - booksellers and stationers

No 27 Parker & Son Ltd - booksellers

On the opposite side of the road is Blackwell's, the world famous bookshop. B H Black-well was opened in these premises in 1879 and generations of writers, poets, academics and Oxford students went to Blackwell's to purchase books to help with their research and stud-ies. Later Blackwell's sold school text books and affordable editions of the classics. Sir Basil Blackwell was known as "the Gaffer" and died in 1984. He was born above this shop in 1889. Blackwell's the original bookshop in Broad Street is still in business and is enormously pop-ular, particularly with students.

Charles Taphouse and Son was established in 1857, closed in 1984.

Charles Taphouse sold musical instruments, records and other electrical goods. In this picture you can see the doors to the many booths where customers could listen to records that they were considering purchasing, similar to Russell Acott (see page 32).

This final Charles Taphouse picture shows a large display of banjo's and guitar's and sheet music. Like many shops of that time, customers were provided with chairs.

Elliston and Cavell, department store was established 1823. The business was taken over by Debenhams in the 1960s and the building extensively rebuilt in recent years.

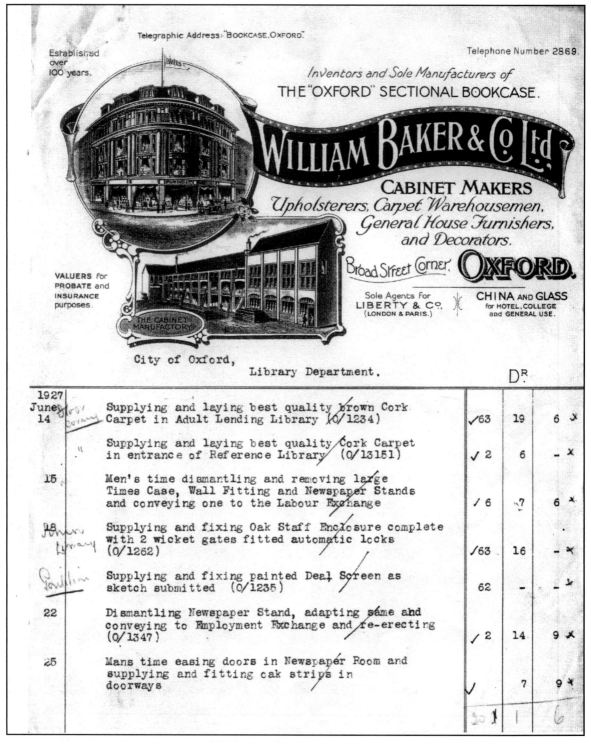

1927					
June 14	Supplying and laying best quality brown Cork Carpet in Adult Lending Library (0/1234)		63	19	6
"	Supplying and laying best quality Cork Carpet in entrance of Reference Library (0/13151)		2	6	-
15	Men's time dismantling and removing large Times Case, Wall Fitting and Newspaper Stands and conveying one to the Labour Exchange		6	7	6
18	Supplying and fixing Oak Staff Enclosure complete with 2 wicket gates fitted automatic locks (0/1262)		63	16	-
	Supplying and fixing painted Deal Screen as sketch submitted (0/1235)		62	-	-
22	Dismantling Newspaper Stand, adapting same and conveying to Employment Exchange and re-erecting (0/1347)		2	14	9
25	Mans time easing doors in Newspaper Room and supplying and fitting oak strips in doorways			7	9
			201	1	6

William Baker & Co. Ltd, sold furniture, china and glassware, they closed their doors in 1987 after trading 141 years. This invoice from 1927 lays out the cost of work done at the City Library.

J Thornton & Son, Broad Street, a secondhand bookshop, now closed, the premises are now used as a café. Inset is a better view of the tiled entrance.

Inside Thornton's book shop - a somewhat haphazard display of their stock.

CHAPTER 11

Turl Street

Turl Street, West side, from Broad Street leading into High Street.

No 18-19 Elmer Cotton Ltd - sports outfitters

No 17 Scout and Guide Shop. My two daughters, Jane and Sally, joined the Brownies in the late 1950s and I bought their uniforms from this shop. The uniform at this time was a brown cotton dress with a brown leather belt, a yellow triangular shaped neck chief and brown leather toggle and brown beret. This shop is still in business in Turl Street.

In St Giles on the Sunday nearest to 11 November, Armistice Day, the scouts, cubs, girl guides and brownies used to march in the parade for the memorial service at the War memorial at the junction of Woodstock Road and Banbury Road. They all looked very smart in their uniforms. The road is closed for this ceremony and lots of people attend to watch the parade, with the mayor of Oxford and councilors followed by members of the British Legion, army, navy and airforce personnel, also sea cadets, army cadets and cadets and officers from the OUTC (Oxford University Training Corp) who use their guns to fire the salute for the two minutes silence in the university park in memory of the men and women who fought and gave their lives for their country.

No 16 Taj-Mahal - Indian restaurant

Ship Street

Jesus College

Market Street. On the corner of Market Street and Turl Street was -

No 4 Emberlin & Son - stationers and printers

No 15 Walters & Co - tailors

No 13 Bonfigllili - art gallery

No 12 Ducker & Son Ltd - hand made ladies shoes. These premises were closed, but Duckers still has a shop at number 6 Turl Street, which still makes hand made shoes.

No 12 these premises are now Rowells of Oxford Ltd. This business was established in 1797 at 115 High Street, as diamond merchants and gold and silversmiths. They were also clockmakers and watchmakers and in their workshop they made the first early pocket watch which is now on display at the Ashmolean Museum in Beaumont Street. Rowells was a family business and was awarded the Royal warrant to the Prince of Wales from 1921 to 1936.

Rowells also owned Ballards the jewellers at the top of Queen Street by Carfax Tower. In 1986 this business moved to 12 Turl Street and the Rowell family retired and the new owners, who were former employees of Rowells, are Mr Stephen Pritchard and Mary Faulkner who are the co owners of this business and are still trading as Rowells of Oxford. They sell domestic silverware which is displayed in the 150 year old hand built mahogany cabinets which came from the High Street premises when it closed. These cabinets are still airtight which keeps the silverware from tarnishing. They also sell antique silver and clocks, pearls and rings.

No 8-10 Walters & Co Oxford Ltd - tailors. This is an old established business selling men's suits, ties and shirts.

No 6 Ducker & Son, established 1898. Duckers was noted as a high class shoe maker making hand made shoes for many well respected customers. They made a special wooden last for every customer, based on the customer's individual foot size and shape, which allows further pairs of shoes to be made when required. They also supplied specialist boots and shoes for rugby, soccer, cricket and rowing as well as footwear for wealthy undergraduates. The famous German air ace, Manfred von Richthofen, more commonly known as the Red Baron, was one of the firm's earliest customers. This shop is still a family business and owned by two sisters who live in Honiton, Devon. The business is run by Bob and Isobel. Bob has worked here for over 32 years making and repairing shoes. One of their customers remarked that her husband said his shoes were so comfy, just like old friends, that he refused to throw them away! Visitors to the shop will be immediately aware of the aroma of new leather.

The photograph of Duckers shows Bob and Isobel, and was taken just after I saw them on a TV news channel about the film "Atonement", which mentioned an actor wearing the famous two-tone brogue tan and white leather shoes made at Duckers.

Walters, men's tailors established in 1887 by Mr F G Taylor and Mr Walters, in December 1985 this shop was merged with Shepherd and Woodward on the High Street.

Ducker & Son, established in 1898, makers and suppliers of high class shoes. Below, Bob and Isobel, Bob has worked here for over thirty years. Stored in the shop are individual wooden lasts for every customer, While many shoes are now made of man-made materials the smell of leather is very reassuring.

CHAPTER 12

The Fallen and the Survivors

Shops which have ceased trading

In this final chapter of my memories of bygone shops in Oxford, I can hardly believe the number of shops that have closed since the late 1950s and 60s and have ceased trading.

Furniture Shops

William Baker, Capes, Davis, Co-operative, Elliston and Cavell, Charles Geddes, Selfridges, Alders, Perrings, Mintys, Webbers and Wards of Park End Street.

Twelve shops, no longer in existence for the purchase of furniture in Oxford.

Grocery Shops

Butlers, Co-operative, Grimbly Hughes, Home and Colonial, Liptons, Maypole International Stores, Twinings.

When supermarkets such as Tescos and Sainsbury's began to trade in Oxford, it quickly brought about the demise of the small shops, as the large shops could buy items in bulk, which resulted in cheaper prices. These small individual shops could not compete. More people were able to buy fridges and freezers, hence more and more were food shopping only once a week instead of daily. When the area of St Ebbes was demolished, the population of this area was rehoused on the outskirts of Oxford and therefore shopped locally. These people had previously been the main shoppers at the small shops in Oxford City.

Jewellers

Ballards, Kirners, Pleasance and Harper, Rogers, Leslie Davey and West.

Hairdressers

Harrisons, Strange (two shops), Godfreys, Del-Nevo (two shops), Maison Gay, Rita Sloan, also hairdressing departments in Fenwicks, Selfridge's, Alders and Elliston and Cavell.

Shops still trading in Oxford

The High Street

Reginald Davis - jewellers

Shepherd & Woodward Ltd - robe makers, men's wear

Payne & Son - goldsmiths

Gill & Co - ironmongers

Turl Street

Ducker & Son Ltd - hand made shoes

Rowell & Son Ltd - watch maker and jewellers, moved from 115 High Street.

Walters & Co (Oxford) Ltd - tailors

Queen Street

Marks & Spencers Ltd.

J. Sainsbury Ltd - grocery store in Westgate Centre

Cornmarket Street

Boots the Chemist

W H Smith & Co Ltd

H Samuel's Ltd

Austin Reed

Broad Street

Blackwells - book shop

Boswells

If you enjoyed this book you might also enjoy . . .

THE CHANGING FACES OF
Oxford Covered Market
Marilyn Yurdan

SERIES
NUMBER
63

. . . or perhaps this book

THE CHANGING FACES OF
Cowley
BOOK TWO

Carole NEWBIGGING *and* Trevor WILLIAMS

. . . or this one

THE CHANGING FACES OF
Headington
BOOK ONE

SERIES NUMBER 5

Christine Bloxham and Susanne Shatford